Jesse Lyman Hurlbut

Seven Graded Sunday Schools

A Series of Practical Papers

Jesse Lyman Hurlbut

Seven Graded Sunday Schools
A Series of Practical Papers

ISBN/EAN: 9783337778811

Printed in Europe, USA, Canada, Australia, Japan

Cover: Foto ©Thomas Meinert / pixelio.de

More available books at **www.hansebooks.com**

SEVEN GRADED SUNDAY SCHOOLS

A SERIES OF PRACTICAL PAPERS

EDITED BY

JESSE LYMAN HURLBUT

Secretary of the Sunday School Union of the Methodist Episcopal Church

———•‑•‑———

NEW YORK: EATON & MAINS
CINCINNATI: CURTS & JENNINGS

CONTENTS.

	PAGE
THE ESSENTIALS OF A GRADED SUNDAY SCHOOL. By Jesse L. Hurlbut, D.D., Secretary of the Sunday School Union of the Methodist Episcopal Church....	5
THE AKRON PLAN. By Hon. Lewis Miller, of Akron, O........................	11
THE WILKESBARRE PLAN. By George S. Bennett, Esq., of Wilkesbarre, Pa.....	33
THE DETROIT PLAN. By Horace Hitchcock, Esq., of Detroit, Mich..........	51
THE ERIE PLAN. By H. A. Strong, Esq., of Erie, Pa.......................	65
THE CHICOPEE PLAN. By Hon. L. E. Hitchcock, of Chicopee, Mass........	79
THE LYNCHBURG PLAN. By Irvine Garland Penn, of Lynchburg, Va.............	90
THE PLAINFIELD PLAN. By Jesse L. Hurlbut, D.D...........................	103
A MODEL SUNDAY SCHOOL ROOM........	113

THE ESSENTIALS
OF
A GRADED SUNDAY SCHOOL.

BY JESSE L. HURLBUT, D.D.

THE living question in the Sunday school of to-day is that which considers its form of organization. As every good public school at the present time is a graded school, so every first-class Sunday school must be. There can be no efficient, regular, and satisfactory work done in a Sunday school without a system of grade.

On this subject there is extensive inquiry, yet general lack of information. The majority of superintendents and teachers have either no conception or at best an exceedingly vague idea of what constitutes a graded Sunday school. We propose in a few words to set forth what are the essential features of a graded Sunday school.

The first essential is that the school be divided into certain general departments, which may be three, four, or five in number. In our opinion the best division is into the four departments— Primary, Intermediate, Junior, and Senior. These departments should exist in reality, as well as in name, and each department should be recognized as a separate element in the working of the school.

A second essential is that of a definite and fixed number of classes in each department. It is not a graded Sunday school where a teacher and her class are advanced together into the Senior Department whenever the pupils reach the specified age. The inevitable result of such a course will be to have in a few years in the Senior Department a large number of "skeleton classes," each with a few members, which is the very evil to be avoided in the graded system. There should be in each department a definite number of classes, proportioned to the size of the school, and this number should be kept uniform. A Sunday school is always "dying at the top," by the loss of its scholars after the age of fifteen years. For this fact there are many causes, some necessary, others avoidable. But, whatever be the cause, it is a fact to be provided for in the management of the school; and the provision should be, not in adding new classes, but in advancing scholars from the Junior Department and filling up senior classes already organized. The classes in the Senior Department should be kept few in number, but kept full in size.

A third essential of the graded Sunday school is that of regular promotions from grade to grade, with change of teachers. It is not necessary for the pupils to pass from one class to another every year in the Sunday school, though this is done in the public school. While a pupil remains in the same department he may continue in the same class and with the same teacher. But when he passes from one department to a higher, or from Junior to Senior, there should generally be a change of teachers. At the period of change from Primary to Intermediate, from Intermediate to Junior, from Junior to Senior, the pupil should come under the care of a new teacher. If teachers are advanced with their scholars the entire system of gradation will be broken up, and the school will be graded in name only.

A fourth essential element is that of stated and simultaneous transfers. The pupils should not be changed from class to class or from grade to grade whenever the superintendent thinks a change should be made. All the promotions should be made at once throughout the school. A "promotion Sunday" should be observed, and provided for long in advance. For three months preparations should be made, the superintendent and teachers should consult, a committee should consider every case, and the changes should be made deliberately and systematically. On one Sunday in the year pupils should be promoted from department to department, and classes should be advanced from grade to grade in the several departments. The basis of promotion should be age, knowledge, and general maturity of character, and the authorities of the school should decide just how much weight should be given to each requirement.

The above are all the elements that we consider essential; but there are also two adjuncts of importance in the graded school.

One is that of a graded supplemental lesson for each department. Some regard this as an essential, and consider no Sunday school properly a graded school without it. We regard it as important, but do not look upon it as one of the necessary features. There is need of a supplemental lesson; it will greatly aid in making the Sunday school efficient, and it should be adapted to the various grades. But the supplemental lesson, valuable as it is, we do not regard as one of the essential features of the graded system.

Another is that of the annual examination. There are a few Sunday schools which require the pupil to pass an examination as the condition of promotion. This follows the analogy of the public school; but in our judgment it is not an essential part of the graded system. The examination in the Sunday school must of necessity be a very easy one, since it is upon lessons studied but little at home and given for a few minutes only once a week. It is apt to be a mere form, and sometimes is only a pretense. While we recommend examinations we believe that they should be left optional, and that the requirements for promotion should be those of age, general ability, and fitness of character. Some reward might be given in the form of a certificate, but it should not be necessary to obtain the certificate in order to receive promotion.

THE AKRON PLAN.

BY HON. LEWIS MILLER.

AFTER an experience of more than twenty-five years with the graded system as carried on in our Akron Sunday school it can with confidence be recommended to others. It embraces the entire school for all this time, but more especially a course of sixteen years which I will try to explain.

Our rooms are a great convenience, and aid much in perfecting the classification; the system, however, can be carried on in any of the present Sunday school rooms; in fact, for a number of years this system was a success in a church at Canton, O., also in the old Akron Church. In each case there was one larger room and but a few separate small rooms.

The classification is based on the age of the scholar; if, however, a scholar seems from some cause to have advanced beyond his age in his general studies, which in most cases is determined by his standing in the public schools, such scholar is put in a class suited to his advancement.

The following analysis will show more definitely the system.

THE INFANT DEPARTMENT

meets in a separate room, fitted for the purpose with elevated seats. Children of about four years of age are received into this department, and remain until they are between eight and nine. Boys and girls are kept together in the same room or class. The class can be of any number; we sometimes reach one hundred and fifty. The class is put in charge of one teacher, with as many assistants as desired. The regular International Berean Lessons are taught, and much time is given to song. In our Missionary Society this department becomes a separate band, with name and motto, making separate contributions, of which proper records are kept.

THE INTERMEDIATE DEPARTMENT

meets in a separate room, fitted similarly to the one described for the Infant Department. Scholars from the Infant Class are promoted into this department when eight years old, or sooner if, in the public schools, they are in the "Second Reader" grade. This class may be of any number; ours sometimes reaches one hundred. Girls and boys are kept in the same class. This department is also put in charge of one teacher, who has such number of assistants as desired. The regular International Berean Lesson is taught in this room, similar in method to that in the Infant Class. The "No. One" Catechism is taught in this department as a supplemental lesson, and it is expected that, before a scholar leaves this room, the Catechism will be thoroughly memorized. A public examination is made before the scholars are promoted out of this department. This, like the Infant Department, becomes a separate missionary band.

THE YOUTHS' DEPARTMENT

meets in the main room, which is provided with a small table for each class; chairs are used; books and papers are kept in the class table, the teacher carrying the key, the superintendent and his assistants having master-keys. Scholars are promoted from the Intermediate Class to this department when ten years old, or when, in the public schools, they are in the "Third Reader" grade. As nearly as possible scholars of the same standing in the public schools are put in classes together, and this distinction is made with scholars of the same age. In this department boys and girls are put in separate classes numbering not to exceed eight, six being the standard. Each scholar is expected to have a Bible and read the story of the lesson. Much attention is given to have the scholar understand and comprehend the simple story as told in the Bible. The regular International Berean Lesson is taught; the lesson book or Berean Leaf is given to each scholar to aid in preparing the lesson. The memorization of the names of the books of the Bible, names of the prominent Bible characters, and sections of the Catechism are required as supplemental lessons. For these supplemental lessons a series of pocket memory lessons is prepared by the school; it is a neat little book, suited for a boy's vest pocket. An examination is made at the end of each year, and the names of scholars having the proper standing are placed on the Roll of Honor. Scholars remain in this department about four years. The younger classes are put nearest the superintendent's stand and, as they are promoted, are moved back each year, the teacher remaining with the same class during the four years. Each one of these classes is a separate missionary band and makes its separate report of missionary contributions.

THE SENIOR DEPARTMENT

classes meet in separate rooms. Scholars are promoted into this department when they are fourteen years old, or when they can show a standing equal to the public high school grade. Boys and girls are put into separate rooms, in which they remain under the charge of one teacher for three years. The class membership numbers from fifteen to twenty-five. The regular International Berean Lessons are taught, more in the analytical form, requiring simple analysis. A blackboard is permanently put on the wall of each room, which affords good opportunity for blackboard explanations. For supplemental lessons the scholars in this department take up the study of Bible history, Bible geography, and sections of the Catechism in suitable form for memory exercises. These classes form themselves into regular missionary bands, taking a missionary field for a name, with suitable mottoes. It is expected that members of these classes acquaint themselves by reading, and by communication with some missionary, with the country and people which they have selected. The classes are socially entertained at the homes of the teacher or parents as frequently as is deemed proper to keep up a social interest.

THE NORMAL DEPARTMENT.

Scholars, when seventeen years old, or sooner if graduates of the public high school, are promoted into this department. The class may be of any number; our classes have averaged about sixty. Ladies and gentlemen are placed in the same class, one teacher having charge. They organize themselves into a regular society, having a simple constitution, and subject to the regulation and direction of the Sunday school society. To the teacher is given the responsibility of seeing that proper decorum is always maintained. As nearly as possible the regular Chautauqua course of normal study is pursued. Regular monthly literary and social meetings are held at the homes of the parents, which aid much to keep up the interest of the normal study. At the end of two years the scholars that have the proper standing on the several written examinations in the normal studies receive, at the annual graduating exercises, suitable diplomas, prepared by the school. The scholars do not understand that they are expected to leave or are excused from remaining longer in the school, but they are only now prepared for a better and higher work. that of teaching and leading others in the good work. Many of these graduates become volunteer teachers ; they join what, in our school, is known as our

YOUNG PEOPLE'S DEPARTMENT.

We have now three large classes in this department, numbering in the aggregate about two hundred. One of these classes calls itself the "Reserve Corps." They are mostly composed of the normal alumni. This class take up the regular lesson one Sabbath ahead of the school and, in regular order, become supplies for absent teachers. They also study the best methods of impressing scriptural truth. The other two classes in this department include quite a number of our young married people. They aim to bring out the higher and deeper thoughts and teachings of the lesson.

THE ASSEMBLY DEPARTMENT

is composed of adult members of the school, meeting in a separate room, under one teacher; the number in the class is not limited. The lesson is here taught more on the lecture plan.

A course of reading has been prepared, suited to each grade, which will give new life and interest to our library, and will enable us, without interfering with the regular lesson study of the school, to impress many things of deepest interest, such as temperance, church government and history, amusements and proper entertainments for young folks, leading them on, step by step, to habits of proper employment of leisure hours.

Our aim is to interest the entire church by

intrusting the educational interests of the church to the Sunday school society, electing many of our oldest members to offices and selecting them as teachers. One of our officers is over seventy years of age, and no one in the Sabbath school takes greater interest or is more efficient, none more acceptable.

The school is regularly organized and governed by the constitution, as approved by the General Conference, and placed in the Church Discipline. Teachers are selected and placed by the superintendent, with the concurrence of the pastor, in the departments to which they are, in the superintendent's judgment, best adapted, and remain with the scholars or class through one department only unless specially changed by the superintendent. Promotions are made only once a year; exceptional individual promotions may occur in some instances.

This system possibly seems complicated and difficult to carry out; we find it simple, easy, and natural, solving many problems that constantly arise in an ungraded school. It especially solves the problem of how to retain our young people in the Sunday school. Our system is thus given in detail in the hope that other schools may profit thereby.

I will add some suggestions for practically working the scheme:

There must be entire unanimity among the officers and teachers in order to successfully start and carry out a graded plan.

First. It must meet with the approval of the pastor.

Second. The superintendent must with the whole heart be in the effort. In fact, he should be, and I believe must be, the prime mover in every step. The superintendent and assistant superintendents in our school during all these years have every year done all of the work of classifying and arranging of classes, made their own "roll," etc. In this way, and in this way only, can they be properly strengthened for the work. They may, if they so choose, call other officers to their aid ; the pastor should, of course, at all times be consulted. The secretary might, in some cases, be of service.

Third. The officers other than the superintendent, are expected to give their full approval and do all in their power, by encouragement and talk,

The Akron Plan.

to aid the work, and, where this cannot be had, secure at least no direct opposition.

Fourth. The teachers have much to give up. The scholars in whom they have taken special interest may be taken away from them. They may not be assigned to have charge of such a class of scholars as they desire; they may be asked to take a place or room which to them for some reason is not agreeable. Fears will be entertained by some that scholars will be lost from the school, etc. All these various objections should be overcome. The aggressive members should have much patience until the teachers are, as a body, at least willing to forego their fears and misgivings and will give the scheme a fair trial. Harmony will nearly always produce enthusiastic workers.

METHOD FOR GETTING A PROPER GRADE.

1. Make an enrollment of the school as follows:

John Brown, Third Reader, age eleven years, March 16, 1892.

Samuel Findley, Fourth Reader, age twelve years, July 13, 1892.

In this way complete the enrollment of the entire school, commencing either with the older or younger scholars, as may best suit: of course those whose ages are above twenty need not be taken; all above that age should be enrolled as married and young people. This kind of an enrollment enables a clear understanding into what class to place every member of the school.

2. Prepare an outline floor plan of the Sunday school room on a scale large enough so that a space can be marked which each class is to occupy, and in each space write the names of the scholars, their ages, the number of the class, and the name of the teacher who is to have charge. For rooms with galleries or without the outline plan is the same. Arrange your plan so as to have all the different class spaces on the same sheet of paper. The diagram on page 23 will give an idea of one kind of room.

A sheet three feet by two and a half will be needed for a school of a thousand members.

3. Having the age and standing in ability on a sheet of paper, outlined as described and illustrated, the next step is to make the selection of

The Akron Plan. 23

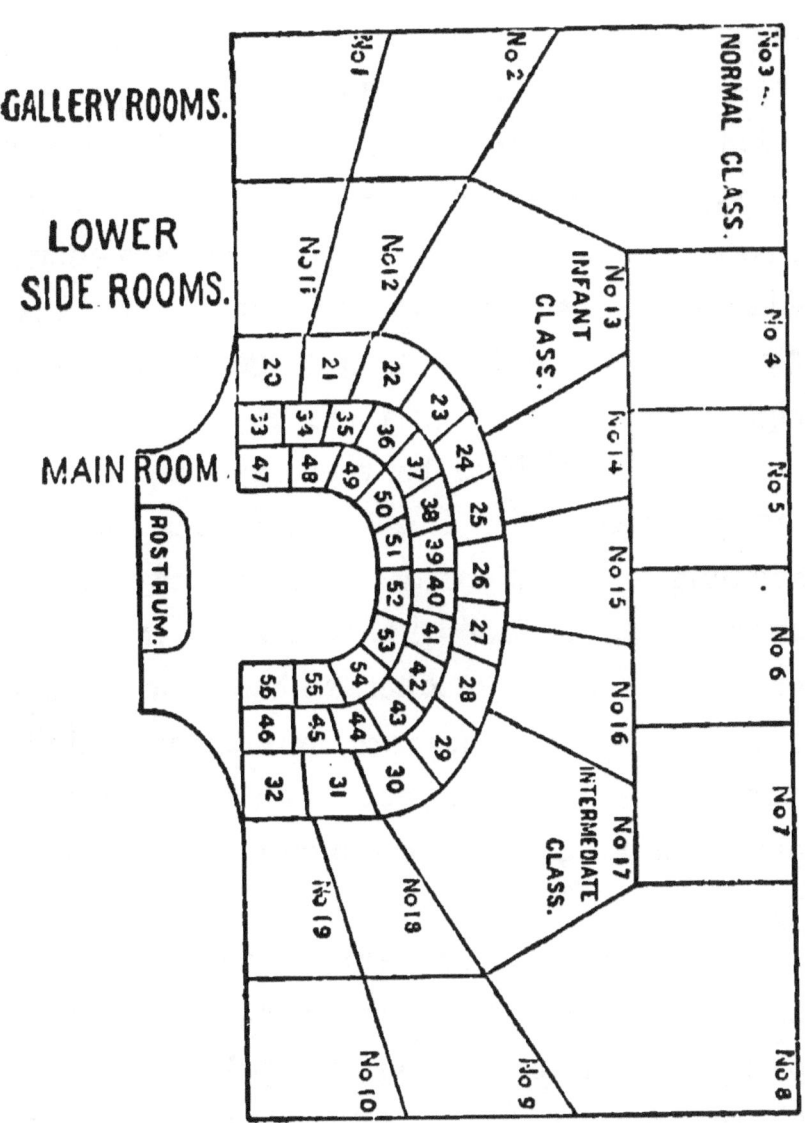

PLAN OF AKRON SCHOOL.

N. B. This plan represents two floors on one diagram. The rooms numbered from 1 to 10 are in the gallery; those from 11 to 19 are under the gallery on the ground floor. The classes numbered from 20 to 56 are not separated by partitions, but are seated in chairs around tables.

the scholars for the different grades and classes they are to occupy. Commencing with the Infant Class, write all the names of the Infant Class scholars into the space outlined for their class. Then place the names of the Intermediate Class in the space outlined for them. These two classes are not difficult to arrange, as all below eight years, boys or girls, are placed in the Infant Class, and those between eight and ten in the Intermediate. These two grades may be subdivided into as many classes as may be desired; in our school we have each of these two grades under one teacher, with one or two assistants. Where rooms are convenient subdivisions by age could be made with profit; we so divide these classes, and sometimes teach them by sections.

The Youth's Department is separated into classes of six to eight members each, and occupies the main room, boys and girls in separate classes, but so arranged that there is a class of girls, then a class of boys, and so on alternately; as far as possible for boys we have a lady teacher and for girls a gentleman. We place the older scholars in the rear of the room, or in the "rear circle," as we say in our school.

The roll of the school now serves an excellent purpose ; select all the boys that are past thirteen years old, but not fourteen, and list them with their standing in the public schools. This is probably best understood by grade, say :

John Brown, seventh Primary Grade, thirteen years, March 6, 1892.

Samuel Jones, seventh Primary Grade, thirteen years, July 24, 1892.

Jacob Smith, seventh Primary Grade, thirteen years, September 16, 1892.

Isaac Miller, seventh Primary Grade, thirteen years, April 20, 1892.

Joseph Crankshaw, seventh Primary Grade, thirteen years, May 19, 1892.

Thomas Marshall, seventh Primary Grade, thirteen years, February 10, 1892.

You will not have much difficulty, in a school of three or four hundred scholars, to find several class lists all in the same grade and same age. This will also permit the selection of certain scholars somewhat in accordance with their social standing. Probably one or two classes of each age will not all stand in the same grade as in the public schools, and there will be others who are not in the public or any other school. The judgment of the superintendent or committee must guide; age probably will be much the best guide, and one, at least, that scholars will recognize and consent to more readily. As fast as classes are formed the names are placed in their locality on the diagram or school room plan. Sometimes, in order to keep the grade by years, the classes may not number six and sometimes may exceed six. All the classes are selected in the same way, a class of boys, then a class of girls, and the names of the scholars placed on the diagram as illustrated.

Scholars above fourteen and under seventeen are comprised in another department, and should be grouped in the same way, only into much larger classes. Where separate rooms can be had fifteen or twenty will not be too many—young ladies and gentlemen separate. In small schools, of course, the classes would be less in number. The age will largely govern in this grade; only such as are advanced ahead of their class will go into higher grades. The names for each class should be placed in the space they are to occupy on the diagram.

The Normal Department is next to be selected. All above seventeen and below twenty that desire to take the course should be put into one class. If a room can be secured large enough fifty to seventy will not be too many. Ladies and gentlemen are placed in the same class. This class becomes an organized literary society, the teacher ex officio president. They meet frequently through the week at some home; a short literary program is arranged and the evening filled up with proper social entertainment. The class may be composed of all the grades, first, second, third, and fourth, on the same plan as the C. L. S. C. readings are arranged, all the grades taking the same studies at the same time, as the studies are so prepared that either may precede the rest. Not all who enter the Normal will probably pursue the studies with such vigor as to undertake the written examinations, of which there should be at least two each year. A good plan is to have all go along with the class, because such as will not do thorough work enough to pass these examinations will, after all, probably get as much good in this class as they would in any other, and the associations are such as will in nearly all cases retain them in the school; and many times, before the final graduation comes, they will make up the required work and finally receive their diplomas. Only those who have pursued the studies and have, with credit, passed the written examinations, should receive diplomas; this gives the proper recognition and is an incentive to study. All who began the Normal work at the same time pass out of the class at one and the same time, unless by special request some one or more remain behind. Those who have not passed the examinations go out without diplomas. In our school we hold to a two years' course, half of the class moving out of the class each year, and new members being promoted into the class. This, it will be perceived, keeps a continuous class, some coming into the class each year and others being removed, either with or without diplomas. With us this plan is working admirably, keeping up a continuous interest.

The Assembly or Post-Graduate Department: The Department of the Young People is divided into a Reserve Corps and a Young People's Class. The Reserve Corps is made up of young people who have passed through the Normal Department and such others as will obligate themselves to act as supply teachers in cases where regular teachers fail; from this class permanent teachers are usually chosen. Other young people's classes are provided for those who do not thus obligate themselves but are willing attendants.

In addition a Young Married People's Class and an Old Folks' Class belong to the Assembly or Post-Graduate Department.

Having thus arranged to place in some department and class every member of the school, and having every name placed on the diagram in the place or class where each scholar belongs, you can study the school members and their varied wants and desires, and so adjust teachers, rooms, and locations and provide for a thoroughly harmonious school. All this work should be done at least a week before promotion day, so that changes can be made after a careful looking over of the scheme of classification. Do not consult teachers or other officers than those who have been aiding in arranging the classification. You must give teachers and scholars to understand that all has been done that is possible in the judgment of the officers for the interest of all the best possible results. Secure from the school a willingness to submit to the judgment of those whom they have placed at the head.

All preparations being completed before the day of promotion, it will not need to exceed thirty minutes after the school is opened on promotion day to place every scholar in the class and department to which he belongs in a school of six to eight hundred scholars. The superintendent, with diagram in hand, remains at his desk, the assistants being his aides. He first calls the names of the Old Folks' Class and asks them to go into whatever room is assigned them; next the Young Married Folks' Class, the Reserve Corps, and Young People's Class, each in order will be asked to retire into the rooms or apartments assigned them. The teachers assigned for these classes will at once be asked to take charge of such classes. The Normal Class members will be asked, with their teacher, to remove into the room assigned them. Then the classes between the ages of sixteen and seventeen, with their teachers, to the rooms assigned them. The assistant superintendents will see that the rooms are in readiness and that the scholars recognize the rooms that they are to occupy. In the same way classes whose ages are between fifteen and sixteen, with their teachers, will be arranged in their rooms or apartments. In like manner the classes between fourteen and fifteen. This disposes of the Assembly or Post-Graduate, the Normal and the Bible or Senior Departments. If in a modern room, with a full suite of apartments, these departments can be asked to close their doors and proceed with arranging themselves for work.

The Youth's Department comes next in order. Every class, section, or desk being numbered to correspond with the diagram numbers, and the assistant superintendents being fully posted as to the order of these numbers, the teachers should be asked to remove to the class place to which they were assigned by the superintendent. The older scholars will be asked first, by reading the names of the scholars who belong to each class separately, requesting them to move to the class to which they were assigned. Read slowly enough to avoid confusion. waiting after the names of a class are read until all are fairly in their places; soon all will understand and the work will proceed rapidly. Having thus called every teacher and every scholar and placed them in their proper classes in their order in the Youth's Department (the whole being done much quicker than it can be told how to do it), this department is set to work; the names of the scholars are carefully ascertained by the teacher of each class, preparatory to making up the class record, then the lesson can be taken up. All children between the ages of eight and eleven are placed in the Intermediate Department and placed under the care of the teacher selected for this division. Then all children under eight years go into the Infant Department. In some schools these last two departments might be placed in one room and a suitable number of teachers provided, so that grading, similar to that of the Youth's Department, might be arranged.

THE WILKESBARRE PLAN.

BY GEORGE S. BENNETT.

THE topic assigned me is a large one. Being a business man I shall not attempt anything theoretical, but shall be as practical as possible. The best way I can serve you will be to give you the result of the effort made by our own school in trying to solve some of the problems of to-day, in the organization, management, and grading of Sunday schools. We have been asked to do this, and in speaking, therefore, of our own school, do not accuse us of seeking only to parade our school before you. We shall give you only the plans that have worked well with us, and tell you of the system and methods employed and now in actual operation in the Sunday school of the First Methodist Episcopal Church of Wilkesbarre, Pa.

It has taken some time and much labor to get our machinery in working order. We do not claim to be pioneers or original. We have taken many of our ideas and plans from others; we have no patent right on our system. What we have is yours, and if we should find anything of yours in this line suited to our use we should not hesitate to appropriate and incorporate it in our own.

CHURCH AND SCHOOL.

We have a short and simple constitution, the form of which can be found in the Discipline of the Church.

The school is a part of the church, and is under the supervision of the Sunday School Board, consisting of the pastor, the Sunday School Committee appointed by the Quarterly Conference, the officers and teachers of the school. The superintendent is nominated annually by the Sunday School Board, and confirmed by the Quarterly Conference. The other officers of the school, male and female assistant superintendents, secretary, treasurer, librarian (who appoints a suitable number of assistants), chorister, organist, teachers of the Primary and Intermediate Departments (who appoint their assistants), and the teacher of the Teachers' Class, are elected annually by ballot of the board. The teachers are nominated by the superintendent, with the concurrence of the pastor, and are elected annually by the board. The school is thus brought under the immediate care and control of the church, and is not a separate or distinct organization. Being thus one department of the church the official board of the church annually appropriates a sum of money sufficient to meet the ordinary running expenses of the school. Extra expenses are met in various ways.

EXECUTIVE COMMITTEE.

We have an Executive Committee of five, elected from among the officers and teachers, with the superintendent as chairman. This committee represents the school in the interim between the stated meetings of the Sunday School Board, conducts all examinations, has charge of all promotions from one class or department to another, the distribution of pupils to classes, and the assignment of teachers to classes.

BUILDING.

The building occupied by our school is one of the finest ever erected for Sunday school purposes. When dedicated, in 1877, Dr. (now Bishop) Vincent declared it to be the most complete Sunday school chapel in the United States, and this, he added, meant the world, for the buildings of the United States for Sunday school use were infinitely superior to those of other countries. It is constructed in the shape of a semicircle and is two stories high. The first, or ground floor, contains a prayer room, church parlors, class rooms, and the library. The second, or principal floor, is arranged especially for Sunday school uses. This is a vaulted room with a gallery running entirely around it. Beneath the gallery, and facing the superintendent, are placed the Primary and Intermediate Departments; their seats are on raised platforms. Large folding doors with glass panels and illuminated Scripture texts shut off these rooms from the Junior Department. The gallery over these rooms contains five large Senior Class rooms. The floors are a series of wide platforms, and chairs are used for seats. Lifting glazed doors, beautifully ornamented with appropriate Scripture texts, shut off these rooms from the auditorium. The main floor is occupied by the pupils of the Junior Department, who sit on chairs grouped around their class tables. The Normal Class sits at one side and the Reserve Corps at the other side, behind the Junior Classes. The superintendent, from his platform, commands a view of the entire school. He can see everyone and everyone can see him and the blackboard behind him. The rooms are so arranged that at the opening and closing exercises the schoolrooms can be made one audience room. The visitors' gallery is behind and over the head of the superintendent, facing the school. The woodwork of the interior is of Southern pine, finished in oil. The entire building is beautifully painted and frescoed, but the decorator's hand is shown more prominently on the walls and vaulted ceiling of the Sunday school room, where the passion flower and grapevine are artistically blended with the Greek and Latin symbols representing Christ. In the arch over the superintendent's desk is a large—

almost life-size—oil painting on canvas, and attached directly to the wall. It is a copy of Hoffmann's celebrated picture, "Christ in the Temple," and is pronounced a fine work of art. The floors are all covered with carpets, which are of colors that harmonize with the wall decorations, and the rooms are seated with chairs, making this Sunday school building unusually attractive and elegant.

GRADING.

Our school numbers 700, officers, teachers, and pupils, with a large percentage of men and women in the Senior Classes. We have most of the modern appliances for Sunday school work, and a most enterprising and faithful corps of officers and teachers. Until within four or five years our school had been divided into the usual Primary, Intermediate, Junior, and Senior Departments, and the teachers had for many years sustained a successful weekly teachers' meeting for the study of the lesson. There were, however, manifest weak points in the work done. The instruction on the part of the teachers, in many cases, was superficial, and there was lack of study on the part of the pupils. The Sunday school had been considered too much as a place where an hour or two could be pleasantly passed on the Sabbath, where the members could be entertained without much work or study on their part, and consequently was of little profit. Our officers and teachers for some time considered how our school might be improved, made more efficient, and more satisfactory results be obtained. A committee was appointed to consider the whole subject. The public school of to-day is looked upon as a model in method and thoroughness of work. While there are many points of difference between the two, yet progressive Sunday school workers have sought to overcome the apparent difficulties, and incorporate, as far as possible, the best features of the secular school.

Some of the members of our committee had been either directors, officers, or teachers of public schools, and thus gave to the subject the benefit of their knowledge and experience. The committee spent considerable time in studying the plans adopted in successful schools—some of the more noted were visited; prominent Sunday school leaders were consulted, and in every way light and information were sought. They in due time made their report, which, after being thoroughly considered and discussed, was unanimously adopted, and the committee were instructed to carry out the recommendations of their report. The committee had a delicate task to perform, to take a school of 700 members and arrange them in the different grades sought to be established. The whole plan was carefully explained to the school, and printed circulars, containing full information, were placed in the hands of the Senior Department, where the greatest changes were to be made. The teachers for the new classes to be formed were first chosen, then the committee met with the other teachers of the classes in the Senior Grade, and by mutual agreement their scholars were permitted to leave any of the existing classes and join any of the new classes to be formed as they saw fit, without the least hesitation or embarrassment either on the part of pupil or teacher. The members of the Reserve Corps were secured by special invitation from the superintendent. The classes of the Junior Department were, with the general consent of their teachers, divided by the committee into the first, second, third, fourth, and fifth years. The committee used their best judgment and made the assignments without examination, general attainments and age being the standards. Transfers were also made from the Primary to the Intermediate, and from the Intermediate to the Junior Department of such as should be promoted. Most of these changes were made on a review Sunday, though some time was previously taken in the necessary detail work, and the transformation was accomplished with the best of feeling, both on the part of teachers and scholars.

We have six grades, Primary, Intermediate, Junior, and Senior Departments, Normal Class, and Reserve Corps.

LESSONS.

The International Lessons are used throughout the entire school. The standard of promotion from one department to another is the age of the pupil, knowledge of the ordinary lessons, and especially of the supplemental lessons studied in each class of the school, with two or three exceptions. These supplemental lessons occupy the first five minutes of each lesson period, and contain valuable information in regard to the Bible and the Church.

THE PRIMARY DEPARTMENT.

In this room the instruction is oral, and the lesson is taught to the entire class by the principal. She is assisted by several ladies in maintaining order, leading the music, marking the roll, taking the collection, noting birthdays, and caring for the wants of the children. The blackboard and visible illustrations are freely used. The children remain here until they are eight years of age. They are taught besides the regular lessons the Lord's Prayer, the Beatitudes, a number of verses of Scripture, and several Psalms. On passing an examination on these supplemental lessons they are promoted to the Intermediate Department.

THE INTERMEDIATE DEPARTMENT.

In this room also the instruction is mainly oral. The children are taught the lesson by the principal, who uses blackboards and charts when needed. She likewise has her assistants, who perform for her the same service as is rendered by the assistants in the Primary Department. The Catechism of the Church, the Ten Commandments and the Apostles' Creed are taught as supplemental lessons. Here the children remain three years, or until they are eleven years of age. On passing an examination on the supplemental lessons they are promoted to the Junior Department.

THE JUNIOR DEPARTMENT.

In this department the boys and girls are assigned to separate classes. As far as possible the girls are taught by male and the boys by female teachers. Each class contains six or eight pupils, who sit around a little table, the drawer of which holds their order of exercises and singing books. The pupils remain in this department five years, or until they are sixteen years of age. These classes are divided into five sections, representing the five years of study in this grade. The pupils of the first section, or year, occupy seats to the right, immediately in front of the superintendent; the pupils of the second year at the left, immediately in front of the superintendent; the pupils of the third year behind the first, and the pupils of the fourth year behind the second. The pupils of the fifth year sit at one side, at the left, and are divided into two large classes for convenience sake, and use for recitation two of the church rooms on the first floor of the building. The teachers go with their classes as they are promoted from year to year in this grade, and when their classes are promoted to the Senior Department they turn back and take new classes from the Intermediate Department.

The pupils of the first year, the most recent from the Intermediate Department, remain in this section one year, and then, if able to pass a satisfactory examination in the names of the books of the Bible and the five doctrines of grace, they may be promoted with their teachers to the second year. The supplemental lessons in this grade are printed on cards and furnished to each scholar. The pupils of the second year remain in this section one year, and then, if able to pass a satisfactory examination in Bible biography from Adam to the Judges, the Apostles' Creed and the Beatitudes, they may be promoted to the third year.

The pupils of the third year remain in this section one year, and then, if able to pass a satisfactory examination in Bible biography of the Judges and Kings, the Ten Commandments, the Great and New Commandments, they may be promoted to the fourth year.

The pupils of the fourth year remain in this section one year, and then, if able to pass a satisfactory examination in the biography of the New Testament, the women of note in the Old and New Testaments and the eight points of Church economy, they may be promoted to the fifth year.

The pupils of the fifth year remain in this section one year, and then, if able to pass a satisfactory examination in Bible geography and history, they may be promoted to the Senior Department.

THE RECEPTION CLASS.

Connected with the Junior Department is a Reception Class for pupils between the ages of eleven and sixteen. All new scholars who join the school and are entitled to enter the Junior Department become members of this class. The teacher makes it her special duty to learn the scholar's age, attainments, home influence and surroundings, and tests his punctuality and regularity of attendance. After the scholar has passed a satisfactory probation he is assigned to a class in the graded system of the school.

THE SENIOR DEPARTMENT.

In the Senior Department the classes occupy three of the five large rooms in the gallery. The members of these classes remain in this grade three years. They study as supplemental lessons "The Chautauqua Text Book Number 19 —'The Book of Books,'" divided into a course of study for three years. Those who pass satisfactory examinations, and who desire it, are promoted to the Normal Class.

There is connected with the Senior Department a Lecture Class, where the lesson is taught entirely by the lecture method. No questions are asked the members. Visitors and strangers are made welcome to seats in this class. There is also a General Bible Class, where the lesson is

The Wilkesbarre Plan. 47

largely taught by questions and answers. These two classes—the Lecture and General Bible Class—occupy large rooms in the gallery, and are for those graduates of the Senior Department who do not wish to fit themselves for teachers in the Normal Class, and for all others of mature years who wish to study the International Sunday School Lessons without entering the graded system of the school.

THE NORMAL CLASS.

The Normal Class occupies seats on the main floor, at the left of the superintendent, during the opening and closing exercises, and uses for recitation one of the church rooms on the first floor of the building, furnished with blackboard and maps. In the Normal Class the regular International Lessons are studied very briefly. For two years the class is taught the lessons of the Chautauqua Normal Union, and passes yearly written examinations on the studies pursued. At the end of two years the members who have passed satisfactorily the examinations on the printed papers furnished by the Normal Union are graduated, receive their diplomas, and are promoted to the Reserve Corps, to be drafted on occasion into the teaching force.

THE RESERVE CORPS.

The Reserve Corps consists of the graduates of the Normal Class and others who are specially fitted for teaching. They occupy seats on the main floor, at the right of the superintendent, during the opening and closing exercises, and use for recitation one of the church rooms on the first floor of the building. The members of this class enter it with the distinct understanding that they will hold themselves in readiness to teach when called upon, and they act, in turn, as substitute teachers for the regular teachers who may be absent. They study the lessons one week in advance of the school, so when asked to teach a class they are prepared by the study of the previous Sabbath. From this class the permanent teachers of the school are generally taken. This fact is a great incentive to diligence and punctuality on the part of the regular teachers, as they know that a number of qualified persons stand ready to take their places if they are irregular or not acceptable.

PROMOTIONS.

Examinations in each department are held during the month of March, by the Executive Committee, and the promotions are all made on one Sunday in April. This promotion or commencement day becomes one of great interest and importance. The members of the Normal Class who have passed their examinations are presented before the entire school by their teacher for graduation. They receive their diplomas from the hands of the pastor, who presents them with words of praise and encouragement. They then take their seats with the Reserve Corps. Promotions from the Senior Department then fill up again the Normal Class. Promotions from the Junior Classes fill up the empty room in the Senior Department. The Junior Classes are all advanced one year, and the Intermediate Department gives a new first year to the Junior Grade. The depletion of the Intermediate Department is then supplied from the Primary Department. The primary room fills up, not by promotions, but by constant accessions made from Sunday to Sunday.

CONCLUSION.

We have tried to give you, as best we could, some idea of our school. We are by no means satisfied with it; there are too many weak places yet to be found. We do not allow, however, our pupils to go on from year to year without learning something, and we afford them the opportunity of gaining much valuable knowledge. We shall continue to labor on in this line and try to make it what its name signifies that it is, a school — a school on the Sabbath for the study of God's word. We have gone into detail in regard to our work that we might help some out of difficulties under which they may labor. If we have dropped a word, or made any suggestions that shall be helpful to Sunday school workers in organizing and conducting their schools, we shall be amply paid for the preparation of this paper.

THE DETROIT PLAN.

BY HORACE HITCHCOCK.

FOR many years, while serving as superintendent of Sunday schools, I saw hundreds of children grow up to young manhood and womanhood, and in a majority of cases go out from the school because they had reached such maturity. Every conceivable effort was made to retain them by securing the best teachers and offering such attractive social influences as could be introduced into a class. Occasionally some magnetic teacher with marked and strong personality would succeed for a time in holding a considerable number of young people in the school, but such teachers were hard to find. The The scholars never seemed willing subjects, but bound in some way to a service that was neither palatable nor in all cases profitable. Why is this so? was the question asked by troubled teacher and superintendent, and too often it was attributed to the perverseness of the young people, and they were given over to the world with the hope that early instruction might have left some seed in their hearts that would in future years bear fruit for their good and the glory of God.

In the midst of these discouraging conditions, which seemed to be almost universal in the Sunday school (so much so that in every institute program was found this topic: "How can the young people be retained in the Sunday school," and when the paper was read and the discussion ended, the mystery was not solved), the writer began to search for the cause that produced these conditions, and asked the question of himself, Why did you leave the Sunday school at the age of sixteen, just as these people do you are so troubled about? Going back to those days and digging out of memory their thoughts, I found that there existed in my mind the thought which was confirmed by the conduct of all schools, that the Sunday school was for children, and not for young people, and that as I was no longer a child I was out of place. It was not that I did not like to be in the school, but that I had changed conditions and the school had not;

therefore was not adapted to me or my wants. This was a revelation which led to the thought that the fault was not in the splendid young men and women who left us, but that of the organization and adaptation of the school to their needs. The conclusion was that if we would retain our young people in the school and church, we must adopt methods and instruction which would be in accord with their age and thought. The public schools at once gave a pattern to be followed. The graded system made some part of the school fit every scholar who came to it, and gave to each one in lower grade a laudable and helpful ambition to reach the higher. This idea, I conceived, might, in a modified form, be introduced into the Sunday school, and as soon as the plan was matured I proceeded to introduce it into the Central Methodist Episcopal Sunday School of Detroit. I will as briefly as possible outline it, trusting it may be helpful to others.

GRADES.

The school was divided into four grades, namely, the Primary, Intermediate, Junior, and

Senior, with two other departments, the Normal and the Home, each one of which was under the direction of a special superintendent, all of whom were under the direction of the general superintendent, the object of this being to make some person who was adapted to the place responsible for the department; and it has proved to be an excellent feature of the graded system, as every assistant superintendent, without any friction with others, has been ambitious to make his or her department as successful as possible.

THE PRIMARY DEPARTMENT.

This grade should consist of all children under eight years of age, under the instruction of a single teacher, with such assistants as are needed. Kindergarten methods of instruction may be introduced to give variety, and by the object lessons used to teach through the eye and by the movements of the body lessons from the Word never to be forgotten. Before promotion to a higher grade scholars should be able to repeat from memory the Apostles' Creed, the Ten Commandments, and the Twenty-third Psalm. The ingenious teacher in this grade will invent a hundred methods for instruction, but before all she must comprehend that she is in the most responsible position in the school. She is laying the foundation for the instruction of the other grades, and as she builds so will the superstructure be strong or weak.

THE INTERMEDIATE DEPARTMENT.

This grade should be made up of scholars promoted from the Primary Grade, and all between the ages of eight and twelve years, and should be divided into classes of about seven scholars each. They should study the same lesson as the Junior and Senior Grades, and in addition to that the Catechism of the Church to which the school belongs. This may be taught by the teacher of the class or by the superintendent of the department. Promotion to the Junior Grade should be made when scholars are about twelve years of age, or upon a test of fifty questions in the Catechism, to be answered in writing, the scholars to pass if forty are answered correctly. This is the test we employ in this grade.

It is important that much should be done for these scholars. Special printed programs and reviews should be prepared for them, and they should receive much attention from the officers of the school. This department should also be a training school for teachers, who should be selected from the Seniors for their fitness for such work and after a pledge has been made that they will attend the weekly teachers' meeting for study and help in methods. These teachers should be promoted with their classes when they show they can do more advanced work. Great care should be taken in the selection of a superintendent. One who is apt to teach will find abundant opportunity to assist both teachers and scholars.

THE JUNIOR DEPARTMENT.

All scholars between the ages of twelve and sixteen should be placed in this grade. In most schools this will be the largest department. The wisest and best teachers should be selected for it, as the scholars are of that age in which we find them restless and difficult to interest. As a rule it will be in the same room with the

Seniors, and should be recognized as a grade as frequently as Seniors. It may be done in many ways, but should be especially in the opening and closing exercises of the school. They may be called upon to read responsively with the Seniors, or to sing the solo part of a hymn while all join in the chorus. Special work may be given them in connection with the school, but not jointly with any other department. If you can keep the Junior Grade busy you can both educate and benefit them. They have great pride in being recognized as a separate organization. The members of this grade should be promoted at the age of sixteen to the Senior Grade. It may be on some examination, but I believe it not best, for this is the point where the boy and girl have gone away from school because they thought they were no longer children and a child's school was not the place for them. Recognize the fact that they are young people as soon as they do. and promote them because they are, into an element that is congenial. At once they are bound to the school by personal pride and by social influences that they are not quick to abandon. Use these elements wisely, and the school has won a victory. The superintendent of this department should be a person whom all the boys and girls like because he is one of them, and while he is "one of them" he should not forget above all things that he is their superintendent, with a responsibility resting upon him to secure their salvation.

THE SENIOR DEPARTMENT.

This most important grade will have in it all persons over sixteen years of age, and all classes should be on an equal footing; that is, that all should be called Senior Classes, whether the members are sixteen or sixty. There should be no "Bible classes."

In the formation of Senior Classes great care should be taken so to adjust them that there shall be no friction. The social idea must be considered, although the scholar should not know that it is being thought of. Scholars who would have no sympathy with each other, and who would never harmonize, should never be placed in the same class; if they are, one or the other will leave the class or school. In the selection of teachers for the Senior Classes great care should be taken. These scholars must be taught, not entertained; so men and women must, if possible, be found who are well informed, apt to teach, consecrated to their work, and who will give to their lesson and class such attention as is required to insure successful work. It is far better in this grade to have a few good teachers with large classes than many teachers, some of whom are incompetent to instruct, and smaller classes. Special instruction should be given in the way of courses of consecutive lessons, lectures, and anything that will supply the intellectual wants of these young people. Never allow the methods of instruction to get into ruts. Teachers should be helped by pastor and superintendent, and nothing should be left undone which would interest and attract the young people. The social element should be employed under careful supervision, but always with the Senior Grade alone. Never allow the children of lower grades to have a part in a social gathering with the Seniors unless by special invitation of the young people. This is the point where they are sensitive, and it must be well guarded.

Employ the young people in every possible way. Let the ruling members of the church recognize them and give them all the church work possible, and they will do it, not only well, but with a spirit that will be inspiring to the church.

Many years of experience convince me that from this department must come the best material for teachers for the school, and will help to settle the vexed question as to where we can get teachers. Take them from the Senior Grade and give them such Normal training as will fit them for teachers and officers. The knowledge that the superintendent is looking among the Seniors for competent persons to fill all places of responsibility is a great inspiration to them, and exalts their idea of the character and usefulness of the Sunday school.

The members of this grade are at an age when they are ready to enter upon some business, and the question as to what it shall be and where they shall get a situation is a very serious one to them. There is no way in which officers and teachers can bind the young people more closely to themselves and the school than by taking a personal interest in their business, and helping them to secure such employment as they need, and securing situations where they will be under good influences.

SUGGESTIONS.

In the Primary Grade a great effort should be made by the teachers to secure a personal acquaintance with the mothers of the children. If possible call at their homes and thereby learn something of their home life, always making a memorandum of such things as impress the teacher as having an influence upon the character of the scholar.

A Saturday afternoon reception for the mothers, who, if possible, are to bring their children, is an excellent method. It should be very informal.

Avoid in this grade, as in all others, the idea of paying scholars by prizes, or in any other way, for efforts made to learn or do what is right, but always keep before them the idea that they are to do well because it is right. This gives the little ones a self-respect which is powerful in its influence.

In making promotions from one grade to another it is not best to have ironclad rules. If a class is to be promoted it is not best to leave one or more out because they have not quite reached the age required. Neither is it wise to insist upon a scholar being promoted because he has reached the proper age, unless he is willing to leave the class he is in.

Promotion may be made once or twice a year. I think once is best, and then it should be at a special service in which all the school should take part.

If a teacher is a misfit in a class the time for promotions is the time to put that teacher where he can work without friction, without giving any publicity to the change. It is also an excellent time to place a scholar not easily controlled with a teacher who is especially fitted to handle him. The scholar should never know why the change was made.

Every Sunday school should have a Normal Class. Courses of study have been prepared which can be handled by any good teacher or pastor who will make an effort. This course will give not only teachers but scholars an exalted idea of the Bible as a book, and prepare them to expound the lessons as they could not without such a course of study. If there is not a class individuals may take the course alone and pass examinations, which will entitle them to the diploma of some of the Sunday school assemblies.

Many superintendents say they cannot grade their schools because they have not separate rooms for the departments. It is desirable to have separate rooms, but if you do not have them you should grade the school, putting each grade by itself in some part of the room, if you have but the one. An aisle or a curtain may be the dividing line. Most excellent results have been realized where the whole school was in one room.

The Home Department is for the benefit of persons who cannot attend Sunday school. The conditions upon which membership is secured are that they shall study the lesson for the day one half hour on the Sabbath; all members to report quarterly whether they have kept the pledge. Those who join this department are members of the school and entitled to all its privileges, such as lesson helps, the use of library, and all other things that other members enjoy. This department should include persons who are distant from the school, the aged, the sick, and may include persons who reside hundreds of miles away, especially those who have been members of the school in other days. This department should have a superintendent who will give it attention and look after all who become members.

THE ERIE PLAN.

BY H. A. STRONG.

THE query often arises whether the modern Sunday school is now at its maximum of efficiency in the line of its development. Wonderful is the progress already attained. The introduction of the International Lesson System marks an epoch. Before that separate schools and even teachers were a law unto themselves. Now schools are in touch one with another; sectarian barriers have been broken down; the unity of the cause is recognized. The Church is one; so are her schools. The culture and the spirituality of the Church catholic everywhere are now the teacher of the teachers. Helps to Bible study are so multiplied and improved that it is difficult to see how an advance step could be taken here. The testimony is well-nigh uncontradicted that the Bible is studied as never before in the light of modern research and science. Teachers, as a body, are measuring up to these privileges and responsibilities.

The advance movement in Sunday school work may not be in its literature, nor in the efficiency or the enthusiasm of its corps of teachers. Elsewhere must we look for the necessity for improvement.

The Sunday school is a school. The expression sounds trite and tautological; but it needs emphasis. Bishop Vincent in his latest book, "The Modern Sunday School," discusses the proposition that the "Sunday school is and must be a school." Out of the fullness of his knowledge and experience proof is there given that the organization, system of teaching, and methods of the public schools must be appropriated by the Sunday school of the day. The modern Sunday school must stand or fall as it is contrasted with the modern public school. By such a comparison alone can excellencies or deficiencies be revealed.

Wonderful has been the development of the public school system in the present generation. Great teachers have appeared in all ages and schools have gathered about them. But this age is remarkable in this, that it has adopted a system of instruction for youth and has trained teachers for that system. The combination of these two elements makes the modern common school system. Let the adults of to-day state the case of their day. Such a comparison would show the value of the present. The great boon from the State to the youth of to-day is an educational system based on scientific principles.

In that system two essentials must be emphasized: first, departments; and, second, the place of the pupil. These departments form a series that are mutually related and dependent. They each mark a step in the development of the mind of the pupil. Again, the pupil has his proper place in that system, assigned not by caprice but by a principle. That principle is the attainment of the pupil in the studies of the system. A competent instructor could find by examination the true place of any pupil in any city public school. Such a statement is so self-evident that it excites no surprise. It is as it should be. The method of assignment and promotion is the public school system. Without it that system would not be what it is.

Apply now these essentials as tests to the Sunday schools. How are pupils there assigned and promoted? The answer must be that such assignment and promotions are there unknown. Here we touch a radical defect and weakness. The statement of that weakness hardly needs elaboration.

As we study further the public school system we find there a course of study. That course of study, comprehensive and complete, the work of educators, is the glory of the system. It is this curriculum that makes its pupils students. In these points also compare the Sunday school.

A summary of these conclusions may be made. The modern Sunday school is not the peer of the modern public school. The Sunday school has a defective system of unrelated, independent departments. The modern public school has a perfect system of correlated dependent departments. The Sunday school has no system of promotions, no training school for teachers, and no course of study. Do its pupils study? Why, they are not required, nor examined.

Is there a remedy for such defects? Could

its department be perfected? Yes; but the disease is deeper than that. Could a system of promotions be devised? Undoubtedly. Could a teachers' class be formed? Many schools have that. To treat these symptoms separately is not to reach the source of the disease. It is but to tamper with difficulties.

The solution lies in a "Course of Study." In the public school the system rallied around a common center—its course of study. All the agencies employed were to render that course effective. Out of a supplemental lesson system will arise conditions that will crystallize into correlation of departments, methods of promotion, a Normal Department with its commencement day, and, best of all, by the help of the home and the church, an atmosphere of study for the scholar without which a school cannot be.

It is believed that such a course of study is practicable. Is it not thus that the modern Sunday school as a school must be improved?

It is evident that the course of instruction in the Sunday school will be different from that of the day school. There, mental culture is sought; here, spiritual culture is the end in view. There, many are the text-books on diverse themes; here, one book and one theme. The Bible and its revelation must be the book and the theme of any supplemental lesson system. It may be taken as an axiom that that system will be the most efficient and acceptable which has the most of the Bible in it and whose teachings best mirror the Bible.

The writer has prepared a series of text-books to be used as a supplemental course of study in the Sunday school. These books have been compiled in connection with his work as superintendent; and as they were completed they were tested in the Sunday school at Erie, Pa. The first one was written five years ago, and since then they have been continuously used.

This school, as now graded, consists of the following departments: Primary, Junior, Senior, Normal, Reserve, and Assembly. The Primary Department has a four years' course and classes to correspond. The Normal Department has adopted the two years' course of study of the Chautauqua Normal Union. The course of study to which attention is directed is an eight years' course—four years for the Junior Department and four for the Senior Department. This course receives pupils from the Primary room at the age of about ten, and, after it is finished, passes them on to the Normal Department.

THE BOOKS OF THE COURSE:*

Junior Department:
    First Year—Catechism.
    Second Year—Catechism.
    Third Year—Life of Christ.
    Fourth Year—Church History.

Senior Department:
    First Year—Jewish History.
    Second Year—Jewish History and the Bible.
    Third Year—Christian Evidences.
    Fourth Year—Christian Evidences.

All these books are catechetical in form, simple in statement, and seek through the questions to give the theme a natural unfolding. They are printed uniform in series. The Junior books have each about twenty pages the size of

---

*These books have been published in pamphlet form by the Methodist Book Concern as "Graded Lessons for the Sunday School."

the Church Catechism, and the Senior books have each about thirty pages.

The Catechism is the first book of the series. Experience teaches that then memory best aids in its mastery. To these text-books on the Catechism is added a supplement on the books of the Bible and its history and geography. The "Life of Christ" undertakes to tell that life in the words of the gospels. "Church History" treats of the apostolic Church and great events in that history, as the Crusades and the Reformation under Luther and Wesley. The first Senior book, "Jewish History," follows mainly the outline of the Old Testament emphasized by the lessons of the international course. The second year book completes that history, and has chapters on the Bible—its translations and geography, etc. The third and fourth years are employed in the study of "Christian Evidences."

A glance shows that the course of study is a study of the Bible, the Junior books being taken from the New Testament, while the Senior cover the Old Testament.

This system calls for regular examination in which the classes of the school participate; it creates an atmosphere of study for the scholars. They are expected and required to study, and they meet that expectation. This system further promotes harmony between the different departments of the school and forms a basis for promotion for the scholars and classes. Promotions are as regular and as judicious as in the public schools.

For what it is, and what it promises, it is brought to the attention of the Church and Sunday school.

THE GRADING.

In this work the number of departments into which the school is to be divided must be fixed. The following will probably be found requisite: Primary, Junior, Senior, Normal, Assembly, and Reserve Departments. The Primary Department may be graded in unison with the school and a course of four years' study be adopted. The Normal Department takes the Chautauqua Assembly course of study. The Assembly is the adult Bible Class of the school. Graduates of the Normal Department constitute the Reserve Department. This department studies the Sunday school lesson a week in advance of the rest of the school, and stands ready to fill the places of absentee teachers. The main body of the school constitutes the Junior and the Senior departments. The course of study is for these Departments, and covers a period of eight years. Their grading is a work of tact and difficulty.

The scholars should be formed into classes, averaging seven to a class. These classes, when organized, should be seated in the school, with the view of promotion from year to year. In a school of five hundred pupils the classes would average about five to each grade.

Where these departments occupy the same room the Juniors may be seated on one side, according to rank, and the Seniors on the other side. The position of the class, being won by merit, becomes a place of honor which the superintendent wisely uses. In the first organization a perfect grade is not attainable. Out of the material given only an approximation to the ideal can be hoped for. Time will cure defects. Each year the entire system moves. With a few annual promotions the actual attains the ideal and the system becomes perfect in its grade. In this we make haste slowly.

THE STUDY OF THE BOOKS.

The time of the introduction of the books and the method of their study are for the decision of the school. A suggestion may be offered. The Sunday school year may follow that of the public school. If so, their study would begin in September, and the examination would be the June following. But, whenever introduced, it should be made plain that the books are auxiliary only to the International System of Bible study. Each session should have an allotted period of time, at least five minutes, for their study. Each teacher can divide the given matter into convenient parts so that the whole may be mastered in nine months. This study will be tested by an examination.

THE ANNUAL EXAMINATION.

This examination is the keystone of the whole system. Without it the course of study is a failure. Its importance must be emphasized before the whole school. How to emphasize it is a problem that each school must solve. A description of the plan adopted in the school where the system originated may throw some light on that question. Some Sunday in June is selected as the day for the examination, and of that day the school is forewarned. Examination questions, twenty in number, and covering the work of the year, are furnished each scholar. These questions are so printed as to leave blank spaces under each question for the answer to be written by the scholar. The whole session of the school is given up to the examination. The papers are gathered and careful work is put thereon in marking the same. Each answer is marked on a scale of 5, and, if the answers are correct, the paper is marked 100. The marks thus make a system of percentage easily understood by all. The minimum percentage to pass the examination is 75. Those who get 75 and upward are known as honor students.

The Sunday following the examination a full report of the work of the school is read. An honor roll of students who pass the examination is placed upon the blackboard or printed in fine form and placed upon the walls of the room.

These honor names are arranged alphabetically and without the percentage of standing, so that it is an equal honor to all students.

The Commencement Day of the graduates of the Normal Class occurs shortly after the examination. These exercises are given on some suitable evening of the week, and are made the event of the school year. After the exercises comes the banquet. For this occasion the Sunday school room is made by the graduates a veritable bower of floral beauty. The Normal graduates and the honor students are received as the honored guests at these festivities.

Such a description may make plain how to emphasize the examination. At least two months before the examination the superintendent should make short, pointed appeals to the scholars and try to fill them with the spirit of study. These examination honors, open to every one, should be made plain to all. Adults work with an object in view. It is the same with the children.

The written examination, its report read to the school, the roll of honor, the promotions, the Commencement and its banquet, are appeals not made in vain to the modern child. What must be the legitimate result of such an appeal to the children? They work for the examination as they do for the examination in the public schools. These last weeks are busy ones. They meet evenings at the homes of the teachers, and on Sunday they gather at the church in special session for class study.

Under such inspiration whole classes have handed in perfect papers. And yet some may and will fail. For them a second examination is given.

Then on the day of promotion the whole school moves forward and occupies the rank won. A course of study can thus revolutionize a school and create an atmosphere of genuine study.

THE CHICOPEE PLAN.

BY HON. L. E. HITCHCOCK.

CAN the graded system be successfully used in small Sunday schools? The plan described in this article has been in successful operation for several years in the Central Methodist Episcopal Sunday school in Chicopee, Mass., in which the membership during that time has averaged 200 and the average attendance has been about 150.

Before describing in detail the plan it may be well to state three principles on which the plan is based:

1. A school, in order to be such, must be instructive as well as evangelistic, and if instruction is to be given there are many principles of instruction which have been worked out in our system of public schools and which have come to be accepted as right principles of teaching anything, and these principles cannot be ignored

in teaching in the Sunday schools any more than they can in the day schools without impairment of the results desired.

2. In general terms, the most important principle of successful teaching is that it should be progressive and adapted in succeeding years to the normal development of the mind of the average child, and this relates to the method of teaching a given subject as well as to the selection of the subjects which shall be taught.

3. Another principle of successful teaching which is of almost as much importance as the one just alluded to is that there shall be one person at the head with a definite plan of work.

Applying these principles to Sunday school work, this school supposes that there is certain instruction which properly belongs to the Sunday school to give; that there is no reason why the Sunday school should not make use of the best methods of instruction which are known to educators so far as applicable; and that when the superintendent is elected to his place the church in effect commits to him or her the entire care of that part of the work of the church, and that it is perfectly proper for him to direct his teachers in the work which he will have done in his school during his term of office.

PLAN OF ORGANIZATION.

The school is divided into three departments, Primary, Intermediate, and Senior. The Primary Department keeps the children until the New Year after they are eight years old; the Intermediate takes them through a ten years' course of study, and then the Senior Department receives them into the Bible classes.

The Primary Department, which meets in a room by itself and has its own order of exercises, is divided into as many classes with separate teachers as may be necessary for the proper care of its little folks, and all under the care of a superintendent of that department. The usual exercises of this department are of the general character customary in such grades.

In July the class which will graduate at the end of the year is formed and placed in the care of a certain teacher, whose special duty is to see that the class is prepared to graduate. The graduating exercises are public, and a neat diploma is presented to each scholar who thus graduates.

The Intermediate Department is divided into ten grades, each representing a year of study and each containing two classes, one of boys and one of girls, although there is no reason why boys and girls should not be together in the same class. There is no division of the Senior Department into grades. It contains only three classes, namely, the Young Men's Bible Class, the Young Ladies' Bible Class, and the General Class.

COURSES OF STUDY.

The principal work of the school is done along the lines of the International Lessons, which are used in all the departments, although the method of teaching them varies in the different grades.

In addition to the International Lessons Supplemental Lessons are taught in the Primary and Intermediate Departments. In the Primary Department these include the Lord's Prayer, the Ten Commandments, the Twenty-third Psalm, the Beatitudes, and the Apostles' Creed.

The following schedule will show at a glance

what are the specific studies of each grade in the Intermediate Department:

Age.	Grade.	International Lesson.	Supplemental Lesson.*
9	I	Learn and recite the memory verses.	First half of Catechism No. 1.
10	II	Same as Grade I.	Last half of Catechism No. 1.
11	III	Learn memory verses and one thought.	Life of Jesus.
12	IV	Study persons (if any) and one thought.	Studies about the Bible.
13	V	Study places (if any) and two thoughts.	Bible Geography.
14	VI	Study manners and customs and two thoughts.	Bible History.
15	VII	Teachings of the lesson having special reference to manhood and womanhood.	History of Christian Church.
16	VIII	Same as Grade VII.	History of M. E. Church.
17	IX	Teachings of lesson bearing directly upon practical Christianity.	Doctrine and rules of the M. E. Church.
18	X	Same as Grade IX.	Government of M. E. Church.

Some explanation of the above is needed:

1. The study of the International Lessons. In all the grades the first things to be learned in each lesson are the title, the Golden Text, and the lesson story, and after these are learned the teachers take up the specific grade instruction

* These Supplemental Lessons have been published by Hunt & Eaton, New York, as " The Ten Minute Series."

as above. The lesson thought, which appears first in Grade III, is carried through all the remaining grades as the central thought for the session. These thoughts are selected by the superintendent, and by him indicated to the teachers at the beginning of each quarter. To illustrate: Take the lesson for September 11, 1892, the title of which was Philip and the Ethiopian. After learning the title, Golden Text, and lesson story the different grades will study as follows:

Grades I and II. Learn the memory verses: 35-38.

Grade III. Learn the memory verses and study thought: "Philip preached Jesus."

Grade IV. Study about the persons: Philip, Candace, the eunuch, and Esaias, and also the same thought as in Grade III.

Grade V. Study about the places: Jerusalem, Gaza, Ethiopia, Azotus, and Cesarea, and the two thoughts: "Philip preached Jesus," and "Prompt response to call of duty."

Grade VI. Study customs: going to Jerusalem to worship, ceremony of baptism, riding in chariot, and the same two thoughts as in Grade V.

Grades VII and VIII. Thoughts—
"Philip preached Jesus."
"Prompt response to call of duty."
"Habit of reading."
"Understand as you read."
"Act up to your knowledge."

Grades IX and X. Thoughts—
"Philip preached Jesus, I can do the same."
"Prompt response to call of duty. How these calls come."
"Fulfillment of prophecy."
"Immediate conversion and baptism."
"The new-found joy."

2. The Supplemental Lessons. The aim of these lessons is to furnish systematic instruction upon the subjects indicated, which are matters that every well-informed person ought to know, but which cannot be taught from the International Lessons. Each year contains thirty-six lessons which can easily be memorized and recited in the twenty minutes usually allowed for this study. The titles readily suggest the nature of the lessons.

A weekly teachers' meeting is held under the direction of the superintendent for the purpose of assisting the teachers in the right understanding of the things required to be taught on the succeeding Sunday, and instructing them in methods of teaching that particular lesson. It is a sort of teachers' meeting and normal class combined.

EXAMINATIONS AND MARKS.

Written examinations upon the International Lessons are held at the end of each quarter, and one upon the Supplemental Lessons is held near the close of the year, upon each of which the scholars are marked. Each scholar is also marked at each session of the school upon a scale of five credits, as follows: one for attendance at the opening of the school, one for attention during school time, one for attendance at closing the school, one for attendance upon preaching service, and one for lesson study at home. These marks, taken in connection with the examination marks and the knowledge of the general work of the scholar during the year, determine his promotion at the end of the year. The scholar who completes the course satisfactorily is awarded the diploma of graduation and admitted to the Senior Department of the school.

No special work other than that usually taken up in Bible classes has been attempted in any of the classes of the Senior Department.

SPIRITUAL WORK.

Although great stress is laid upon the work of instruction in the school, it must not be concluded that the spiritual work is overlooked. This is attended to in two ways: first, in the lesson thoughts in connection with the International Lessons, which are selected, as far as possible, to enable the teachers to illustrate and enforce spiritual truths; and, secondly, each teacher is expected to do all she can in the way of personal example and influence to bring the members of her class to Christ. Of course, if any special religious interest at any time in the church seems to call for it, the work of the school is suspended and all the energy is brought to bear upon the evangelistic part of the work.

RESULTS.

The actual working of this plan has demonstrated that many things which might seem to be objections have been only imaginary. At the start the scholars were classified according to their ages, with occasional modifications with reference to their places in the public schools, and the teachers were placed in the different grades with reference to their relative abilities, and they were asked to teach certain specific things, which of course they cheerfully did. The scholars, who are accustomed to this method in the public schools, at once caught the idea, and their parents became interested to see that their lessons were learned before coming to the school. The attendance of teachers became more regular, for each teacher, having his own specific work to do, very soon realized that if he were absent his work could not be fully done by a substitute, and the attendance of the scholars was much improved, for they could see actual advancement from Sunday to Sunday.

The attendance of scholars in the Intermediate Department averages fully twenty per cent more than in any other department. Of course, the adoption of any system of graded work means considerable work for a superintendent at the start, and this to a busy man is a serious matter; but after the system is fairly started it works easier and with less friction to annoy than any other plan, and the cause is worthy of the effort required.

Two reasons why schools should be graded may be given: 1. Children will be interested in what they can understand, and if the instruction both as to form and substance is adapted to their growing intellectual abilities it will easily be received and taken care of, while, on the other hand, if it is not comprehended it excites no interest in the mind of the child, and he is glad to get out of the school as soon as he can.

2. The teachers do not go on with their classes from year to year indefinitely, and by this means it is possible to bring ten succeeding classes under the teaching of the ablest teacher you can get in a particular grade, instead of confining that able teacher to only one class for ten years. There can surely be no question as to which is the better course.

THE LYNCHBURG PLAN.

BY IRVINE GARLAND PENN.

IT was early in the year of 1890 when it became a positive fact, to the superintendent who is now leading our Sunday school, that we had accomplished practically nothing as a school during the twenty years of our existence. In this school our superintendent was entered when but a lad of five years. He had shifted from class to class, not by reason of any promotion by the superintendent, teacher, or any other officer of the school, but as he advanced in age from five to eight, eight to ten, and ten to fifteen years he correspondingly grew in size, and of his own free will and accord he moved from class to class, with no other recommendation for promotion but age and size. At the age of fifteen he was made secretary, and in that official capacity he took account of the pennies collected, disbursing them as the board might order.

Our future superintendent was then promoted to be the teacher of Bible Class No. 3. It was not Class "Three" because its members knew more or less than Class 1 and 2, but because its members were a class of misses, while Classes 1 and 2 were masters and young men. In fact, Class 3 was as much entitled to be Class 1 as Class 1 was to be Class 1. He was then promoted to his present position. His career is related in order that it may be shown that the conclusion which he had reached was founded upon personal experience and observation, which he took no account of then, but which served to demonstrate more forcibly to him that the Sunday school was accomplishing nothing save the one fact that it met on Sunday mornings ostensibly for religious instruction. It must be said, however, in justice to other superintendents, that, whatever inclination he had to seek and ascertain the defects and best needs of the school, he was led slightly in that direction by those who had shown that something was needed, and who knew that a change must take place if our Sunday school would maintain her standing as a large and growing one in the community. We numbered four hundred, in round figures, and while during the boyhood of our superintendent the corps of teachers were not efficient, by reason of the lack of advantages necessary to proper qualification, yet when he came into office he found himself surrounded by a corps of teachers nearly all of whom were prepared by intellectual and divine strength to teach anything that could possibly be put into a Sunday school course with propriety.

No longer were there "blind leaders of the blind" in the school, but intelligent leaders in mind and heart. It was a proposition that needed no demonstration to our superintendent that he now had the opportunity to present the one thing needful in the school, namely, method and system in instruction and the adaptiveness of work to the susceptibility of the pupil, which is the essence of the grade idea. As soon, then, as this idea was clear, our superintendent at once began inquiry and to hunt literature bearing on this subject.

"The Modern Sunday School," by Bishop J. H. Vincent, was the first book consulted, and the first sentence of Chapter XII, on Gradation, gave the idea which settled the conviction. The sentence reads: "The Sunday school is a school." Nothing is truer than this one sentence, and the sooner our superintendents and teachers get this one idea ineradicably fixed in their minds the better it will be for our Sunday school interests. Most assuredly the "Sunday school is a school" to teach the things of God, to instill his truths and impress his good deeds and loving favors to the children of men upon the mind and hearts of those who must grow up in the admonition of the Lord, if they would make valiant soldiers and good citizens. It was evident that our Sunday school was a school, though poor in order, poor in work, and poor in everything but singing and the giving of picnics. Dr. Vincent's book was further consulted, with others, and our superintendent reserved several months to mature his plans and present them.

In the meantime several articles in the "Sunday School Journal" of May and September, 1890, greatly helped him. A plan of action was finally decided upon; first a new registration, giving name, age, educational fitness, and some minor matters, was gotten of each pupil as accurately as possible. In the meantime our plan had by this time been told the school, and the taking of a new registration, preparatory to the gradation, created a genuine revival of interest in the work. And, too, when the fact was known that the school was undergoing a change which would give larger and better opportunities to the children, fathers and mothers who could not themselves read, but who knew what it was to have John and Mary to go from Catechism to Catechism, from class to class, every time higher and higher, gave vent to their feelings in many "Amens" and "God-bless-yous." To these expressions of approval and the prayers of this class the success of our system may be greatly attributed.

The registration having been taken, our superintendent was intrusted with the gradation of the school. On the one hand the burden was light; on the other heavy. The labor was light, for no amount of it could seem a burden, so great was the interest in the four hundred souls who were now for once to be put into the shape of an ideal Sunday school.

On the other hand, it was for once a burden to do duty as he saw it, because there were large boys and girls who had been hitherto neglected in this ghost of a school, and now had to suffer the worry of doing a thing over when it might have been done well at first. But our superintendent had no time now to indulge in sentimentality; the work was to be done, it was given him to do, and he knew it was for the best good of the school; hence he went at the work in the fear of the Lord. During three weeks of incessant prayer and labor the work was done, submitted to and approved by our board. What a change to be made during the next Sunday! John, who could not read, used to be in Bible Class No. 1; now he is to study the Catechism.

During the next Sunday the grading was done, classes rearranged, teachers replaced to suit the departments; and after all was done we looked calmly upon the scene, and never in all the history of our Sunday school did it look so well, and never have we seen children with such bright and happy faces as were in that school on that morning. It will never be forgotten even by the smallest pupil. As I have said, they were always good singers, but with new life in them they sang the praises of God on that morning until it seemed we were all tasting of the riches of God as never before. The three departments arranged were Primary, Intermediate, and Normal, with provision for a Normal Training Class. It may be said here that we have seen the necessity very clearly for the introduction of a Junior Department or Course on account of the length of our now existing departments. This will be done on "Promotion Sunday" after our January examination.

A course of study was carefully arranged to cover the three departments, consisting of seven years: Primary Course (provided child entered at the age of three), ages from three to ten years; five years' Intermediate Course, ages from ten to fifteen years; five years in the Senior Course, ages from fifteen to twenty years. These departments, and the years in each, will be slightly modified by the introduction of the Junior Course.

The course embraces in our Primary Department the International Lessons in the form of the "Picture Lesson Paper." The Lesson Paper is, however, not taken up until the pupil has been in this department for four years, presuming that he enters at three years of age. The lessons during the first four years are orally taught, and consist of selected verses of the Bible, Lord's Prayer, Beatitudes, and selected portions of Catechism No. 1. Since the day school system only admits pupils at six and seven years, it is presumed that they are not prepared to be classified in any way as students of the International System on account of their inability to read.

Thus all of the pupils from three to six years are put into one class and taught orally, as explained above. There are sometimes exceptions to this general rule in the case of children who may have had early training around the fireside.

The pupils in the Primary Department, having received the Lesson Paper at seven or eight years, have only from two to three years to remain there before the proper age is reached, all other things being equal, for their transfer to the next department. During the last two or three years of the Primary Course the pupils have for supplemental lessons selected Psalms and verses, Catechism No. 1 to Question 25, inclusive. It has been demonstrated to our board in our promotions that this Primary Course is well conceived and serves admirably well the purpose intended, which is to lay a foundation upon which a structure might be reared without fear of tottering.

In our Intermediate Course the International study begins the first year with the "Beginner's Leaf" and is used during three years of the five years' course. In the remaining two years the "Berean Lesson Leaf" is used. In the use of the Beginner's and Berean Leaves the course of teaching is laid down by the Examining Board, and the teacher directs her talk and instruction in that direction. This is to avoid what may be termed "splatterdash" teaching—the teaching of everything with special reference to no one particular thing, the teaching of what is understood and not understood. The supplemental lessons for the Intermediate Course include the Ten Commandments, Catechisms Nos. 1, 2, and 3, and the Old Testament read and thoroughly considered from Genesis to Numbers, inclusive. In this department special effort is made to impress the Baptismal Covenant, the Ten Doctrines of Grace, Ten Points of Church Economy, etc.

The pupil is now fifteen years of age, and, all things being equal, he is ready for the Senior Course.

In this department the "Senior Lesson Quarterly" is used. The supplemental work consists of a completion of the Old and New Testaments thoroughly read and considered during the five years. In addition to this, McGee's "Outlines of the Methodist Episcopal Church" is studied the first year; "The Teacher Before His Class," by James L. Hughes, in the second year; "Normal Outlines for Primary Teachers" in the third year; "History of the Sunday School," by Chandler, in the fourth year; Discipline of the Methodist Episcopal Church, and "Christian Baptism," by Bishop S. M. Merrill, in the fifth year.

Our pupils are then entered in the Normal Training Class, where they read such books as "Open Letters to Primary Teachers," by Mrs. W. F. Crafts; "Hand Book for Teachers," by Dr. Joseph Alden. They also consider more fully the doctrines of our Methodism and the history of "that great religious movement," as one has termed it. The pupils of this class subject themselves to much training for Sunday school teachers. They are permitted and are expected to meet the teachers in their weekly meetings in order that they may go over the lessons with the teachers and be prepared in case of an emergency. Our examinations are held semiannually. In the supplemental work the examinations are conducted in written form. As to the International studies, the recommendation of a pupil by a teacher is sufficient to determine his work and his ability to pass to a higher grade. The teachers conduct their own examination and make tabulated results, the whole of which is submitted to our Examining Board, consisting of eight members, who carefully pass upon it and order the promotion. The promotion is then made by the superintendent according to the tabulated results.

As an encouragement to pupils we have found it wise to issue certificates to everyone as they complete the course of study of each department, and finally, when the Senior Course is completed, to issue a diploma. The assembly idea also obtains in our school as a part of our system. This has been found indispensable as an incentive to devotion, because it makes our higher Intermediate and Senior classes feel their importance in a measure when they are called together every fortnight to hear some talk or paper upon some religious topic, apart from the Primary and lower Intermediate classes. In order that the teachers might be more thoroughly interested in the success of the system, and thus influence their children, our superintendent has very wisely introduced the social feature into our work, and very often in our consideration of Sunday school matters we find ourselves in the midst of a pleasant and agreeable reception. This has worked well, for we are all creatures of humanity with the same innate social tendencies. The day of days, yes, the red-letter day, is "Promotion Sunday." These Sundays will never be forgotten. The enthusiasm is equal to that of Children's Day in every respect. Boys and girls with eager hearts pass from class to class. As a means necessary to the success of our system our superintendent very carefully presented the necessity of a larger library than we had. The plans for raising the money were arranged, and, to use the popular expression, "they worked like a charm." Hundreds of dollars were raised, with which we now have over one thousand volumes and a neatly built library case of twenty feet in length. It would be a pleasure to tell how that money was raised.

As to the results accomplished in our school by the system, suffice it to say they are manifold. Order, system, interest, care, study. regular and punctual attendance by officers and teachers, have been some of the results. In conclusion, let us pray that our superintendents and boards will see the necessity for this system in their schools, and that before long the schools of our Methodism may be one of continuous gradation.

THE PLAINFIELD PLAN.

BY JESSE L. HURLBUT, D.D.

TWO years have passed since our Sunday school was graded, and the results of the system are now so apparent that we can safely recommend our plan, for it has met and endured the test of time. Our Sunday school, before the grading was accomplished, embraced about four hundred scholars of all ages, with an average attendance of two hundred and seventy-five. Its officers and teachers were fifty in number. It was by no means an ideal school, though above the average in the efficiency of its work and the interest of its exercises. Its building, however, is a model of convenience and adaptation to the work of the Sunday school, having around the main hall eighteen class rooms, all capable of being either secluded or opened together at a moment's notice.

We found in our Sunday school certain evils and defects, all of which may be seen elsewhere. Some of these were: 1. "Skeleton classes" in the Senior Department, consisting of four or five scholars, being the remains of what had once been large classes of boys and girls. 2. A constant tendency among the young people to fall away from the school after reaching the age of sixteen or eighteen years. 3. Great discrepancies of numbers in the classes; large and small classes side by side in the same grade. 4. In almost any given class a lack of unity in the age and the intellectual acquirements of its members. 5. Great difficulty in obtaining suitable teachers for new classes, or to take the places of teachers leaving the school.

After many conversations a conclusion was reached that most of these evils might be removed, and others of them might be lessened, if the school were reorganized according to a good system, and then maintained as a thoroughly graded school. A committee was chosen to prepare a plan. Correspondence was held with graded schools, all printed information was carefully studied, a plan was prepared, printed, submitted to the Sunday School Board, discussed, modified, and finally adopted unanimously. The following are the principal features of the plan, for which we make no claim of originality. as each of its elements was already in successful operation in one or more graded Sunday schools:

1. That the school should be arranged in four general departments: The Senior, for all over sixteen years old; the Junior, from ten to sixteen years; the Intermediate, from eight to ten; and the Primary, for the children younger than eight years. These divisions are not arbitrary, but represent the average standard of age, to which exceptions might be made in special cases.

2. In each department the number of classes to be fixed and invariable, except that in the Junior Department there might be some necessary elasticity in the number of classes, owing to the varying number of scholars promoted into the department in different years.

3. Promotions to be made annually, and all at the same time, on the last Sunday of March.

Except in special emergencies no changes in classes to be made during the year, either by teachers or scholars. If a teacher accepts a class on "Promotion Day" it is generally to be considered an engagement for the entire year, unless a necessity arise.

4. While in the same department a teacher and his class to be advanced together; that is, from the first year of the Intermediate Grade to the second, from the first year of the Junior Grade to the second, etc. But the promotion from one department to another to be attended with a change of teachers, in order to keep the same number of classes in each department, especially the Senior Department, from year to year.

5. While special supplemental lessons may be provided for each department, the promotions to be made upon general fitness, age, and intelligence, and not upon the result of an examination. No examination upon the plan of the public schools is practicable in the Sunday school, where all the classes are studying the same lesson. All attempt at making an examination the prerequisite of promotion is apt

to become a pretense in the actual working of the scheme.

6. It was also decided that the entire school should be reorganized on a certain day, in accordance with the above plan. A careful committee of seven members, including the pastor and superintendent, made a canvass of the school, ascertained the age of each scholar under seventeen, conferred with the teachers, and then prepared a new list of teachers and scholars for all classes in the school, making many changes, both in the teaching staff and the assignment of scholars.

Sunday, March 30, 1890, was a memorable day, being our first "Promotion Sunday." We approached it with some anxiety, for on that day our committee held in its hands the fate of every teacher and every scholar. Old ties were to be broken, new relations were to be entered upon. Ten teachers were to be returned to the ranks as Senior scholars, and the complexion of every class was to be changed. No one could tell what heart-burnings would be engendered and what disappointments would come. The superintendent made a statement of the new plan, and proceeded to read the new roll, beginning with Class No. 1 of the Senior Department. As the names were called the members left their former classes and took their new places in the class room. Eight classes were assigned to the Senior Grade, each having a separate room. These classes were a young men's class, three young ladies' classes, a class of elderly ladies, a lecture class of ladies and gentlemen, a class of reserve teachers, and a normal class to be trained for teachers in the course of the Chautauqua Normal Union.

In the Junior Department sixteen classes were formed. Those of the lowest rank, the first year, took the front row of seats; the second year the second row, etc. Those of the fifth year Junior were in two classes, one for boys and another for girls, each having a room. The teachers of these two classes remain constant, and change their scholars every year; but during the first four years of the grade the teachers advance with their scholars, changing their seats every year, but retaining their classes.

The Intermediate Department consists of two large classes, each in a separate room. One class is of little children just promoted from the Primary Department; the other, of those who have been in the Intermediate Grade a year. The teacher remains with each class for two years, the term of this grade. We are inclined to favor a three-year term in this grade, with a class for each year, thus making the age at admission to the Senior Department seventeen instead of sixteen years.

Our Primary Department formerly consisted of nine or ten small classes under one Primary superintendent. In the reorganization we constituted it as one class, with a teacher and an assistant. This change released a number of teachers for service in the school, and was on the whole an improvement. Whether it would be desirable everywhere depends on circumstances. In many places it might be easier to find ten teachers, each of whom can teach ten scholars, than one who can teach one hundred.

When the roll of the school had been fully called every teacher and every scholar had been assigned, except one boy, who had joined the school that day, and was left standing in the middle of the room in a bewildered state of mind over the revolution which was going on around him. A view of the newly arranged classes from the platform showed the school looking more orderly than ever before, and gave it the appearance of having twice as many adult scholars as formerly.

One item must not be forgotten. The superintendent announced that each department would hold a "reception" adapted to the age of its members. The Senior reception was appointed for Monday evening of the next week, and was to include upon its program music, addresses, readings, cake, and cream. All the young people were eager to be counted in, and hence willing to leave their old classes for the new ones. A fortnight later the Junior Department held its reception, with a stereopticon entertainment and the refreshments. Even if a boy can obtain a superabundance of cake at home he will be drawn by the prospect of another slice to the Sunday school sociable. Each department held its own reception, all were happy, and the young ladies and gentlemen were not made to feel that they were simply on the fringe of an institution adapted mainly to little children.

The Plainfield Plan. 111

The system thus inaugurated has been in operation two years. What have been its results?

There were at first some complaints by teachers, scholars, and parents. But only one teacher left the school; the classes settled down to work and soon became acquainted; a few changes, but only a very few, were made in the assignments of the scholars, as, for example, where a mistake had been made in the age of a pupil; and soon everybody was satisfied with the new arrangement. Among its manifest benefits we may note the following:

1. The Senior Department is maintained with large classes and growing numbers. There is a social feeling, an "esprit de corps," in a large class which is not found in a small one; hence the shrinkage is less. And whatever loss is met is more than supplied from the new blood infused each year on "Promotion Sunday."

2. The scholars in the Junior Department have an aim and a hope before them. They look forward to their promotion with earnest expectation, and are on this account the more loyal to the school.

3. Inasmuch as all changes are made at a

given time they are prepared for. For three months the superintendent is planning for "Promotion Sunday." If a teacher can be better fitted with a class, a change is made at that time; and where many changes are made at once the friction of each is reduced to a minimum. Classes are made more nearly uniform in their constituency, and the school is kept up to an evenness of organization which greatly increases its efficiency.

4. There has been a marked increase in the membership of the school. Notwithstanding the organization of a mission school by the church, taking away several workers and some scholars, the school has an attendance from seventy-five to one hundred larger than that of two years ago.

After a trial of two years we are sure that the establishment of a graded system and a faithful adherence to its plans have greatly benefited our Sunday school.

A MODEL SUNDAY SCHOOL ROOM.

THE Sunday school is the door to the Church through which enters the great majority of its members. This fact alone would account for the increasing interest that the Church now manifests toward the school. As the institution which trains the young for the Church, and leads both young and old into the Church, the Sunday school is entitled to the Church's support and care.

The housing of the Sunday school is one of the most important subjects that can come before the Church as the guardian of the school. Too often the work of the school is impeded by unsuitable and inconvenient quarters. Just as the public school building now claims the attention of architects and sanitary engineers, the Sunday school hall is also attracting notice.

It is only twenty-two years since the first

building thoroughly adapted for the uses of the Sunday school was erected at Akron, O. This building, the joint conception of the Hon. Lewis Miller, superintendent, and Mr. Jacob Snyder, architect, has furnished most of the ideas peculiar to Sunday school construction, and is therefore entitled to preeminence in the record. Others have improved upon the details of the Akron plan, but its fundamental principles have never been superseded, and can never be. Those principles are only two, and they seem almost incompatible with each other. They have been called "aloneness" and "togetherness;" that is, that each class in certain departments shall be isolated in a separate room, and yet that all the classes may be brought together into one room for general exercises without delay, without confusion, and without the change of seats by the classes.

Among the dozen or more Sunday school buildings on the Akron plan one of the most convenient and most complete, yet not one of the most expensive, is that connected with the Methodist Episcopal Church in Plainfield, N. J. As this was for twenty years the church home of the Rev. Bishop John H. Vincent, the Sunday school bears the appropriate name of "Vincent Chapel." The plans were drawn by Mr. Oscar S. Teale, architect. Mr. Teale was at

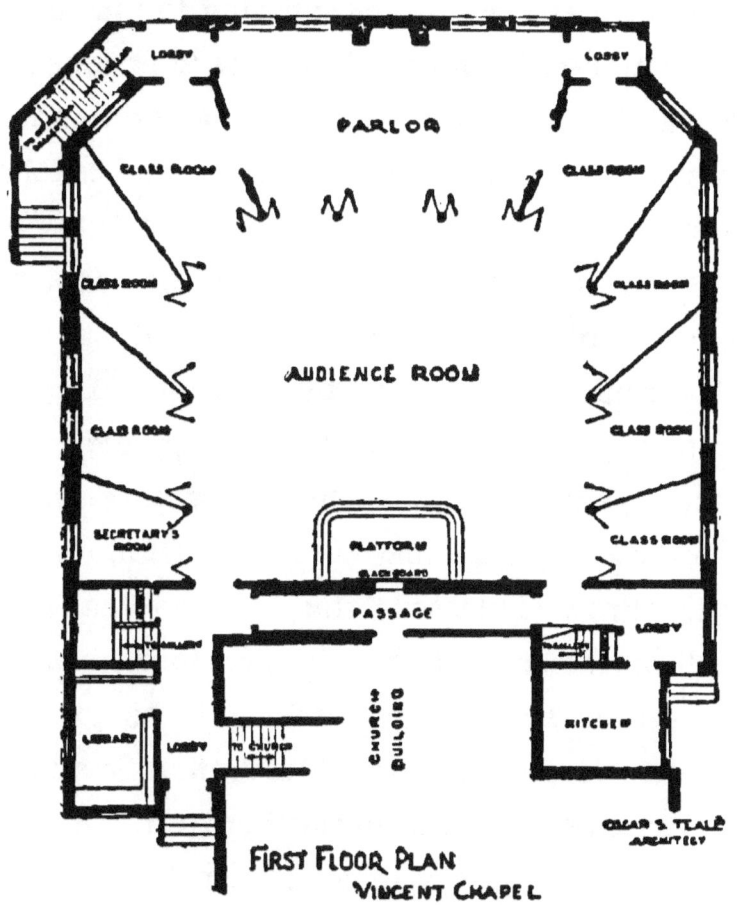

FIRST FLOOR PLAN
VINCENT CHAPEL

that time the efficient secretary of the school, and added to an architect's knowledge a worker's practical acquaintance with the needs of the Sunday school. The chapel, as may be seen by the diagrams, embraces a large room, with eighteen smaller class rooms around it, nine upon each floor. The partitions of the class rooms are so arranged as to offer no obstruction to the line of vision from any seat in the building to the superintendent's desk and the blackboard fastened to the wall back of it. Thus the superintendent can see and be seen by every pupil and teacher in the building. He can also be heard with perfect ease in every class room, as the acoustic properties of the building are excellent.

The main room is used by the Junior Department, in which the scholars are from eleven to sixteen years of age. The classes are seated according to grade, the "first year Juniors" on the front row of classes; the "second year Juniors" on the second row, etc., for four rows, the boys on the superintendent's right, the girls on his left. Each year, on "Promotion Sunday," the classes move one row farther from the desk, and the new classes formed from the Intermediate Department take the front row of seats.

The nine class rooms on the ground floor are used as follows: In the left-hand corner, just where the most of the scholars pass in entering and leaving, is the secretary's room. Next is the "fifth year Junior," into which all the girls enter after four years in the Junior Grade, leaving their former teachers for a new one. In this class they stay either one or two years, according to age and acquirements, and from it are promoted to the Senior Department. The third room is that of the "Ladies' Bible Class;" the fourth, the "Reserve Class." Next comes the church parlor, seating a hundred people, and used by a large Senior Class. The next room is for the "first year Intermediate," that is, those just advanced from the Primary Department; the seventh, the "second year Intermediate;" the eighth, a "young men's Senior Class;" the ninth, and last, the boys' section of the "fifth year Junior," the largest class of boys in the Junior Department.

On the ground floor are four entrances, one at each corner. As the chapel stands at the rear of the church it was necessary to have the principal entrance on each side of the room facing the school. This is a slight drawback, as a rear entrance would be preferable, in order not to distract attention to the late comers.

The partitions between the class rooms are windows of ground glass of amber color. They are movable, so that classes can be united whenever desirable. Those between class rooms and the main room are double doors of ground glass, so hung that they may be swung aside easily, and arranged when open not to interfere with the line of vision. All the rooms are well lighted and well ventilated; and the main room, when all the rooms are closed, has abundant light and air from a clear story above, with movable windows.

To the gallery and its classes there are three entrances. The one from without the building leads exclusively to the Primary Class, which, by having its own exit, can adjourn earlier than the rest of the school. The two other stairs are interior and lead to the gallery corridor, on which all the class rooms of the upper floor open. These are separated from each other and from the main room by sliding doors of amber glass, so that they may be united or isolated at will, and in a moment. The seats in these classes rise in tiers so that those in the rear as well as in the front can see the platform and the blackboard. There are nine class rooms, of which the central one is for the Primary Department, and all the others are for the Senior classes. All the Senior classes are large, and

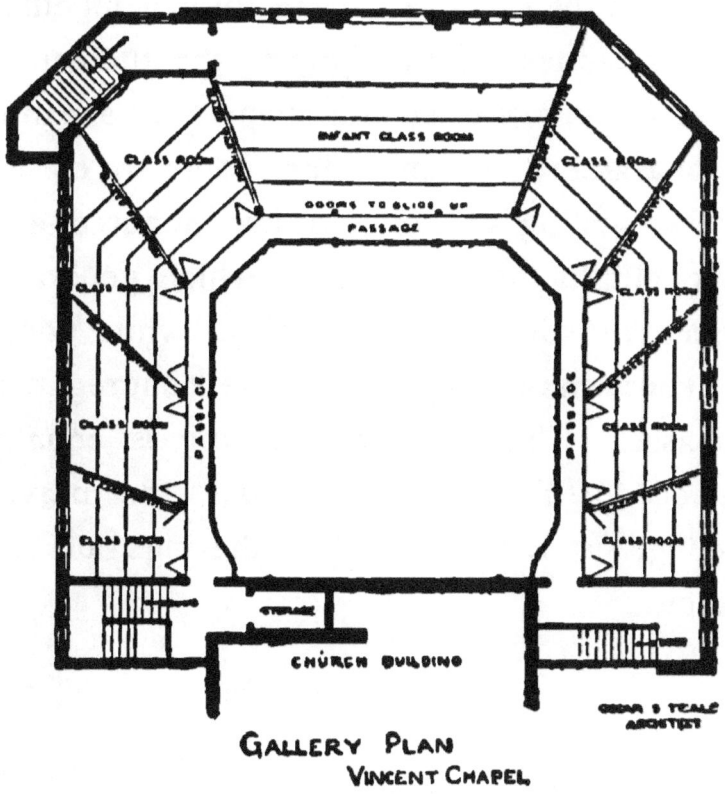

GALLERY PLAN
VINCENT CHAPEL.

are kept full by promotion every year from the Junior Grade.

The library room is at the main entrance, so that books may be delivered by the pupils while passing into the school, and might be given to them while passing out, though in fact they are brought by the librarian to the classes. On the opposite side of the building, in the rear of the entrance, is a kitchen, which is used at entertainments and social gatherings. For these two or three of the class rooms are thrown together as a refreshment room adjoining the kitchen.

One advantage of such a chapel is its expandable character. When all the rooms are closed there is seating capacity for two hundred and fifty chairs in the main room, which generally suffices for the prayer meeting, while room after room may be opened as the congregation increases. This form of building is equally adapted for the Sunday school, the prayer meeting, and the social gatherings of the Church.

THE END.

www.ingramcontent.com/pod-product-compliance
Lightning Source LLC
Chambersburg PA
CBHW020129170426
43199CB00010B/695